W9-DDG-995

The Let's Talk Library™

Let's Talk About Living With a Parent With Multiple Sclerosis

Melanie Ann Apel

The Rosen Publishing Group's
PowerKids Press™
New York

With love to Tristan Ottenfeld, my little buddy. Melanie

Published in 2001 by The Rosen Publishing Group, Inc.
29 East 21st Street, New York, NY 10010

First Edition

Book Design: Maria Melendez

Photo Credits: pp. 4, 11, 12, 16, 20 © International Stock; pp. 7, 15 © FPG International; pp. 8, 19 © Index Stock Photography.

Apel, Melanie Ann.
    Let's talk about living with a parent with multiple sclerosis / Melanie Ann Apel.
        p. cm.— (The let's talk about library)
    Includes index.
    Summary: This book discusses what multiple sclerosis is, the symptoms of the disorder, the types of therapies used in treatment of MS, and the ways children can help a parent who has MS.
    ISBN 0-8239-5621-0
    1. Multiple sclerosis—Juvenile literature. [1. Multiple sclerosis. 2. Diseases.] I. Title. II. Series.
2000
616.8'34—dc21

Manufactured in the United States of America

Table of Contents

Nick's Mom

One morning, Nick's mom woke up feeling very strange. At first, she could not feel her legs. She tried to get out of bed, but her legs were weak. They could not hold her up. She got scared. Nick's dad took his mom to the hospital. A doctor talked to Nick's mom about how she was feeling. The doctor ran some tests. He found something wrong. Nick's mom had a **disorder** called multiple sclerosis.

◄ *This woman felt sick so she went to see her doctor. He ran some tests and found out she had a disorder called multiple sclerosis.*

What Is Multiple Sclerosis?

Multiple sclerosis, or MS, is a disorder of the brain and **spinal cord**. People who have MS have nerves that do not work well. This is because there are **scars** on the cells of the **nerves**. There is **tissue** on the nerves that help control the brain and spinal cord. When the tissue gets **inflamed**, scars form on the cells of the nerves. The scars destroy the covering on the nerve cells. If there are scars on the nerve cells, the nerves cannot help people move their bodies.

People with MS can have trouble moving their bodies. Sometimes they might not even be able to get out of bed. ▶

Who Gets MS?

People who get MS usually start having **symptoms** when they are between 20 and 40 years old. About 35,000 people in the United States have MS. More women than men have MS. People who live in northern areas are more likely to get MS, though it is not clear why. If someone in your family has MS, there is a greater chance that you will get it. Scientists do not know what causes MS, so they cannot say that **heredity** is what makes MS more common in some families. It may have to do with where people in a family come from or what they eat.

◀ *People who live in northern areas are more likely to get MS. Doctors do not know why this is so.*

Symptoms of MS

People who have MS usually have certain symptoms. They might feel weak or dizzy. They might lose their balance easily, feel cranky, or have trouble seeing. Some people with MS feel their symptoms most of the time. Others feel their symptoms only once in a while. Symptoms of MS can come and go. Many people who have MS can still work and take care of their children. Others become so sick that they have trouble doing most things. They may end up needing a wheelchair to get around.

Scientists are not sure why some people with MS have mild symptoms while others get very sick. This man is still able to ▶ work and get his son ready for school.

Treating MS

Although there is no cure for MS, there are medicines to treat the disorder. Some medicines slow down the nerve damage caused by MS. Other medicines are used to treat the symptoms of MS. Medicines can be taken by mouth or through shots. If a patient has bad headaches, for instance, he or she can take pain medicine to help with that symptom. Scientists are trying to come up with medicines that will actually repair some of the cell damage that MS has caused.

◀ *Some medicines treat the symptoms of MS. Other medicines slow down the nerve damage caused by the disorder.*

Therapy

If your parent has MS, he or she might go to **therapy**. It could be speech therapy, physical therapy, **occupational therapy**, or all three. Therapy can help your parent do things that have become difficult because of MS. Speech therapy helps a person speak more clearly. Physical therapy helps people keep their bodies strong. This type of therapy can also help people walk better. Sometimes people become less **coordinated** because of MS. Occupational therapy helps people have better control of their hands.

Going to therapy is a great way to deal with having MS. ▶

Alice's Dad

Alice is on the soccer team at school. Today is the last game of the year. Alice wants her dad to come watch her play. Her dad has MS, and today he feels very sick. He wants to see Alice play soccer, but when he feels this bad he cannot get out of bed. He tells Alice how much he wishes he could watch her game. He says he will be thinking of her the whole time. Alice leaves for the game with her mother and older brother. She smiles at her dad. Still, she cannot help feeling sad.

It's hard when your parent is too sick to watch you play ◀ *soccer or do other things. Just remember that he or she will be thinking of you the whole time that you are playing.*

Dealing With Your Feelings About MS

When your parent has MS, it can also be hard for you. You might feel lonely or mad. Talk to someone about your feelings. You can talk to a friend or to a teacher. You can even talk to your sick parent. Just make sure you think about his or her feelings, too. You should also remember that the two of you can still do things together. You can watch TV or listen to music. You can sit quietly and talk about your day. What is important is spending time with each other.

Talk to your mom or dad about what you are feeling.
It will make both of you feel better. ▶

Helping Your Parent Who Has MS

If your dad or mom has MS, there might be times when he or she needs extra help. Offer to help cook dinner. Take out the trash. Keep your room extra clean. Sometimes just understanding that your mom or dad is not feeling well can be a great help. Let your parent know how much you love him or her. Knowing you care will go a long way in making your parent feel better.

◀ *One way to help your parent with MS is by keeping your room as clean as you can.*

Glossary

coordinated (koh-ORD-in-nayt-ed) When something works together in a smooth way.

disorder (dis-OR-der) A sickness or medical condition.

heredity (her-ED-uh-tee) The passing of physical or mental traits from one generation to another.

inflamed (in-FLAYMD) When something is sore or swollen.

nerves (NERVS) The part of your body that connects the brain and spinal cord to the rest of the body.

occupational therapy (ahk-yoo-PAY-shun-al THER-uh-pee) A type of treatment where people learn to use their hands to do small tasks.

scars (SKARZ) Marks left by healed cuts or sores.

spinal cord (SPY-nul KORD) The thick, whitish, cord or nerve tissue in the backbone or spine.

symptoms (SIMP-tums) Signs of something.

therapy (THER-uh-pee) The treatment of disorders or injuries.

tissue (TIH-shoo) The substance that forms the parts of living things.

Index

The Same Person Inside

Even when people are sick, they are still the same inside. Your dad might have MS, but he is still the same smart, funny, loving person he has always been. He is brave, too. Dealing with MS is not easy. It takes a lot of strength to handle being sick. Tell your dad that you are proud of him. Let him know that you are on his side. Help out when you can. All these things will keep him going when times are tough. Working as a team will help keep you close, too. With love and hope, you can handle whatever problems come your way.